# Thomas Willson

## Mister Carbide

Michael Webb

Copp Clark Pitman Ltd.
A Longman Company

ISBN 0-7730-5160-0 (Casebound) ISBN 0-7730-5161-9 (Paperback)

**Canadian Cataloguing in Publication Data**
Webb, Michael, 1949–
Thomas Willson, mister carbide

(Scientists & inventors series) Includes index.
ISBN 0-7730-5160-0 (bound) ISBN 0-7730-5161-9 (pbk.)

1. Willson, Thomas Leopold, 1860–1915 — Juvenile literature. 2. Calcium carbide — Juvenile literature. 3. Electrochemical industries — Canada — Juvenile literature. 4. Inventors — Canada — Biography — Juvenile literature. 5. Chemical engineers — Canada — Biography — Juvenile literature. I. Title. II. Series.

T40.W54W4 1991 j660′.92 C91-094538-1

MICHAEL WEBB, a former school teacher and chemistry professor, now works as an editor and writer in Toronto. He has a doctorate in chemistry from the University of Alberta.

EDITING AND PHOTO RESEARCH: *Melanie Sherwood*
SERIES DESIGN: *Susan Hedley*
LAYOUT AND ART DIRECTION: *Liz Nyman*
TYPESETTING: *Sonja Mills Graphic Arts Inc.*
PRINTING AND BINDING: *Friesen Printers Ltd.*

ACKNOWLEDGEMENTS
Special thanks to Francesca Verre, aged 12, and to Grace D'Alfonso for reading the manuscript.

PHOTO AND ILLUSTRATION CREDITS
*Alcan Aluminum Ltd.:* 8; *Board of Education for the City of Hamilton, Archives:* 3; *Canadian National:* 15; *Canapress:* 1; *Cyanamid Canada Inc.:* 10; *Cyanamid U.S.:* 23; *Steve Demeter, Panavision:* 5; *Ford of Canada Archives:* 19; *The Linde Organization:* 22; *Mary Evans Picture Library:* 7; *Metropolitan Toronto Region Conservation Authority:* 4, 14; *National Archives of Canada:* cover 53498, iv 53499, 11 C53493, 17 53483, 20 C53491, 21 C53500; *National Capital Commission:* 24, 25; *New York Convention and Visitors Bureau Inc.:* 6; *Office of the Development Commission, City of Woodstock:* 2, 16; *Ontario Hydro:* 13, 18; *Springs Industries Inc., South Carolina:* 9; *University of North Carolina, Office of University Relations:* 12.

Copp Clark Pitman Ltd., 2775 Matheson Blvd. East, Mississauga, Ontario L4W 4P7
*Printed and bound in Canada.*

# Contents

*Thomas Willson.*

# INTRODUCTION

Thomas Willson was one of Canada's greatest inventors. In his lifetime, he became very famous. Today, he is largely forgotten.

Willson took many risks in his career. As a young man, he failed again and again. But he never gave up. Good luck brought him his greatest discovery and earned him the nickname "Carbide." Then he earned and lost a fortune.

*Willson's greatest discovery is still used in industry.*

# Childhood

*Woodstock today.*

Thomas Leopold Willson was born on March 14, 1860, on a farm in Princeton, near Woodstock. Woodstock was in Upper Canada, now known as Ontario.

The Willson family was well-known in Upper Canada. Thomas was the grandson of the Honourable John Willson, who served in the Upper Canada **legislature** for 26 years. Thomas's father was a **minister**. Thomas's mother was an artist and musician.

Thomas's father was kind and generous. But his efforts to help a friend landed the family in trouble. He used the family farm to **guarantee a loan** for his friend. When the friend failed to repay the loan, the Willsons lost their farm.

They moved to Bridgeport, Connecticut. There, Thomas's father opened a factory. It failed, and the family moved back to Canada. Thomas's father died when Thomas was only 14. His mother then raised her three children in Hamilton, Ontario.

Thomas owed his mother a great deal. She worked terribly hard to support the family. She gave guitar and painting lessons, and even rented out a room in their house to help make ends meet.

*Thomas studied at Hamilton Collegiate Institute.*

# First Inventions

In high school at Hamilton Collegiate Institute, Thomas loved science. He did well at **physics** and **chemistry**. He enjoyed doing experiments and even set up his own **laboratory** in the basement of his home. His mother was not amused. When Thomas left school, his mother told him to find somewhere else to do his experiments.

Thomas started work for a local **blacksmith**, John Rogers. They agreed that Thomas could use the loft above the blacksmith's shop to do experiments in his spare time. Before long, John Rogers was helping young Thomas with his scientific work.

*A blacksmith at work.*

*An arc light.*

Thomas was already fascinated by electricity. The use of electricity was still in its early stages. Around the time that Willson started work, a famous American inventor, Thomas Edison, was developing the modern light bulb.

Willson built his own dynamo to make electricity. This machine was driven by steam. He used the dynamo to run an arc light, which he hung in the loft window. We are used to light bulbs that have a glowing wire inside them. Arc lights did not have this wire. The light came from an electric spark that jumped across a gap.

Reliable arc lights had been around for over 30 years. But Willson's electric light was the first in Hamilton. Thousands of people came to see it. The arc light gave Willson his first **patent**, when he was almost 21.

# Failure

Willson felt ready for bigger things. He found a way to drive a string of arc lights with his dynamo. Then he got orders from a hotel and a factory for his lighting system. But he was trying to move too quickly.

He installed his lighting system before it was very reliable. The orders were cancelled because the lights would often blink on and off, or go out altogether. The loss of the orders was a major blow. Willson was in debt and saw no future in Hamilton. In 1882, he moved to New York City for a fresh start.

*Modern New York City by night.*

*The penny-farthing was a strange-looking bicycle.*

He worked very hard there and did not have much time for hobbies. But he did like cycling. He rode a bicycle that did not look like the ones you see today. This strange machine was called a **penny-farthing**.

Over the next few years, Willson had several jobs. In one of them, he developed arc headlights for trains. But he wanted to be his own boss, so he did experiments in his free time. Then, at age 26, he started his own electric light company. It failed, and Willson again had to work for someone else.

Willson must have been disappointed, but he did not slow down. His various jobs gave him all sorts of experience. The most important was the work he did with **furnaces** powered by electricity.

# Trying to Make Aluminum

In his mid-twenties, Willson had the idea of using electric furnaces to make aluminum. This metal is very common now, but in those days it was very hard to make. Willson was determined to change that.

*A modern mill.*

He began to experiment with his electric furnace in 1888. Then, in 1891, he met Major James Turner Morehead. The Major owned a **cotton mill** on the banks of the Dan River in Spray, North Carolina. The river supplied **hydro-electricity** for the mill. Willson learned that the river could make more electricity than the mill needed. And the Major was very interested in electric furnaces.

Willson set up the Willson Aluminum Company in Spray and built an electric furnace there. He used the furnace to heat mixtures of chemicals to try to make aluminum. He failed every time, and the future of the Company looked very bleak.

Also, unknown to Willson, other inventors had already found a new way to make aluminum. Even if he had succeeded in making it, he might never have made any money from his invention. Then, when all seemed lost, a customer asked Willson to make another metal, calcium.

*Making aluminum today.*

# A Lucky Accident

*A modern furnace.*

Willson came up with a plan, which his helpers tried on May 2, 1892. They boiled **lime** and **coal-tar** until the mixture was dry. Then they poured the mixture into Willson's furnace over a period of two hours. The furnace heated the mixture to over five thousand degrees Celcius – nearly as hot as the surface of the sun!

They took some of the hot mixture from the furnace and dropped it into a pail of water. Willson hoped that the water would bubble violently and turn milky. Calcium makes water do this. The bubbles form because calcium and water make a gas, called hydrogen.

Sure enough, the water bubbled and turned milky! But something did not make sense. A strong smell, something like the smell of garlic, filled the room. Hydrogen gas has no smell, so what gas was in the bubbles?

One of Willson's helpers tried burning the gas. He used a burning rag fixed to the end of a fishing pole. Every time he moved the rag over the pail, the gas burst into flames. Willson knew that hydrogen burns with a pale blue flame and does not make any **soot**. But the new gas burned with a white flame and made lots of soot.

Once again, Willson failed in what he set out to do. Since the gas was not hydrogen, then the material from the furnace could not be calcium. What on earth was it? The answer to that question made Willson a rich man.

*One of Willson's furnaces.*

Willson found better ways to make the new material in his furnace. He sent samples to the University of North Carolina and to a very famous scientist, Lord Kelvin, at the University of Glasgow in Scotland. After a few months, he learned what he had made. The dark brown material from the furnace was *calcium carbide.* The gas it formed with water was *acetylene.*

*Part of the University of North Carolina.*

*Burning acetylene.*

Willson found out more about these materials. He learned that he was not the first person to make them. A German scientist had first made calcium carbide 30 years earlier. He had also made acetylene from it. But Willson had found a much cheaper way to make them.

Before Willson's discovery, a kilogram of calcium carbide would have cost over twenty thousand dollars to make! Willson could make it over a million times cheaper, for about two cents a kilogram. For the first time, people could think about everyday uses for calcium carbide and acetylene. As the word of Willson's discovery spread, someone gave him the nickname "Carbide." It stayed with him for the rest of his life.

Willson had been interested in lighting since he had built his first arc light. He hoped that the bright light from burning acetylene would change the world and make him rich. To protect his future, he took out more patents.

# Sunshine at Night

*These lamps used kerosene.*

At that time, electric lighting was still in its early stages. There were no really good ways to light a home at night. One of the best had come from another Canadian inventor. He was Abraham Gesner, a doctor from Nova Scotia. In the 1840s, he had found a way to **distil** lamp oil from coal. He called his oil *kerosene*. Burning kerosene gave more light and less smoke than burning candles and **whale oil**.

*Railways transport many materials.*

Some cities made their own gas supplies for gas lamps in homes and on streets. But the lights were quite dim. The light from burning acetylene was about twelve times brighter. Gesner impressed people when he first showed them the light from a kerosene lamp. Now Willson could amaze them with the light from burning acetylene.

The flame from kerosene looked yellow. Burning acetylene looked like sunshine. In fact, scientists found that plants grew almost as well in the light from acetylene lamps as they did in sunlight.

But candles and kerosene had an advantage. Acetylene is a gas, and gases are harder to handle and **transport** than solids and liquids. Willson worked at making solid and liquid acetylene by cooling the gas. Also, he thought about making acetylene where it was needed and not transporting it at all. It could be made anywhere from calcium carbide and water.

# Fame and Wealth

*Willson had this house built in Woodstock.*

Like Willson, many people thought that acetylene would become the main gas used for lighting. Willson and Morehead made lots of money by selling the rights to make calcium carbide and acetylene by Willson's method.

Within five years of Willson's discovery, eight carbide factories opened in the U.S., but seven of them went broke. Acetylene did not catch on for home and street lighting in the way Willson had hoped. Some people thought that the smell of acetylene was too unpleasant for home use. So, Willson and others worked hard to find more uses for the gas.

Meanwhile, Willson was making good use of his money. Above all, he wanted to help his mother. In 1894, he bought land in Woodstock. He had a beautiful house built there. Of course, it had a laboratory in the basement. When the house was ready, he sold it to his mother for a dollar.

*Mary and Thomas with one of their children.*

In 1888, he had met a young woman, Mary Parks, from California. He was determined to marry her. But, for several years, she would not agree. At first, she thought he was ugly and too **formal**. It is true that he was shy all his life and had few close friends.

They finally married in California in August, 1895. The next year, they moved to Canada, where Willson planned to build his own carbide factories.

# Back in Canada

At first, the Willsons lived in St. Catharines. Thomas was building a factory in nearby Merritton. Like all his factories, it had to be close to a large supply of running water. The furnaces depended on hydro-electricity.

*This hydro-electric station makes electricity from running water.*

When the factory was complete, the Willsons moved to Woodstock to live with Thomas's mother. Thomas and Mary soon started a family. They raised three children, two sons and a daughter.

The Willsons were already rich, and the factory in Merritton was a success right away. They made even more money when Willson sold his U.S. patents to the Union Carbide Company. This has since become one of the world's largest companies. By 1990, it had 44 000 employees around the world and customers in over 100 countries. And it all started from "Carbide" Willson's chance discovery.

There were more and more uses for acetylene. It lit the lamps on bicycles, cars, and miners' helmets. Even lighthouses used acetylene lamps at sea. Willson himself supplied the acetylene lamps for the carriages on Canadian trains.

*The headlights on this old car burned acetylene.*

# The Explosion

"Carbide" Willson had enough money to retire early and live very comfortably. But he always wanted to push ahead. In 1902, the family moved to a house in Ottawa. It is no surprise that Willson built a laboratory in the basement. By 1904, he had two more carbide factories. One was on Victoria Island in the Ottawa River, the other in Shawinigan, Québec.

A customer of his Ottawa plant was the town of Maxville, Ontario. The town bought frozen acetylene to run its street lights. Willson's businesses were booming. But then an accident threatened the whole future of acetylene.

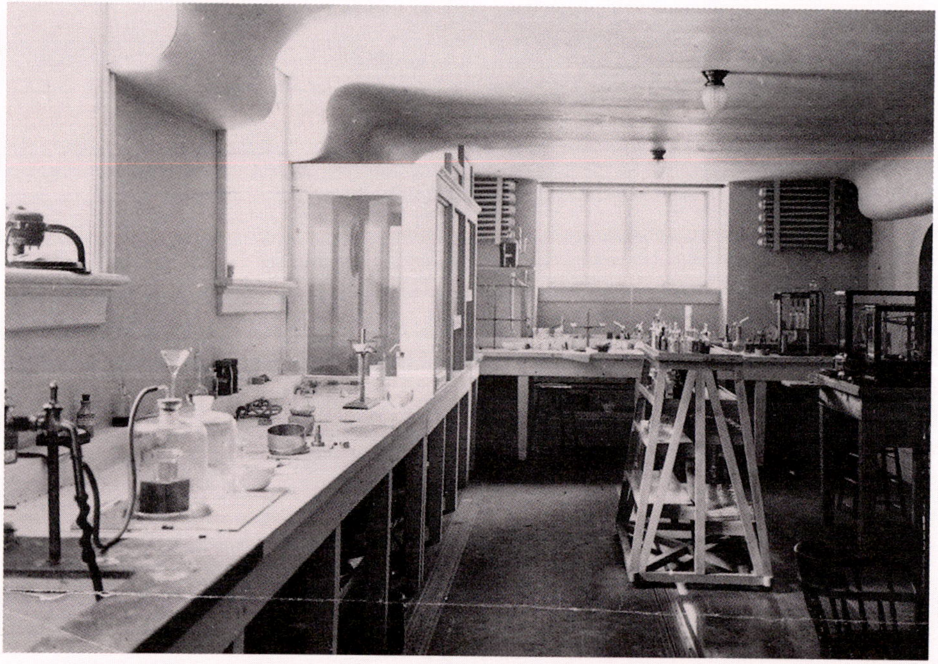

*Willson's laboratory in the basement of his Ottawa home.*

*Willson invented this much safer marine buoy.*

For some time, **marine buoys** with acetylene lamps had helped boats find their way safely. The buoys on the St. Lawrence River had large storage tanks for acetylene gas. A small boat, *The Scout*, refilled the tanks as the gas was used up. But one day in April, 1904, something went horribly wrong.

*The Scout* was at the dock in Kingston, Ontario, refilling three buoys with acetylene. One buoy blew up and set off the other two. *The Scout* was badly damaged. The captain and three of his crew were killed. People were suddenly very nervous about using acetylene.

# Greater Success

*This welder is using an oxyacetylene torch.*

Willson turned this accident into another success. He designed buoys that did not need to be refilled with acetylene gas. Instead, they made their own. Each buoy had its own supply of calcium carbide and an automatic way of adding water to it. Willson's new buoys were very safe and reliable. He built a big factory in Ottawa to make them. They were used in many parts of the world.

*Most farms use fertilizer.*

But the greatest success for acetylene was its use in cutting iron and steel. This use began in France in 1903, with the invention of a torch that burned a mixture of oxygen and acetylene. The flame was hot enough to cut through metal plates. Today, we take these "oxyacetylene torches" for granted. For example, we see workers using them on building sites.

Before this century, it had been hard to cut iron and steel or to connect pieces of these metals. Thousands of bolts and **rivets** held together such big structures as ships and bridges. But oxyacetylene torches could **weld** pieces together. Ships, bridges, big buildings, and heavy machines became easier and faster to build. The torches were used to make and repair cars, which were first **mass-produced** in 1908.

Again, Willson did not want to stop working. He had heard that hot calcium carbide took in nitrogen gas from the air. The result was a good **fertilizer** called "cyanamide." So, he was hard at work in his basement trying to make other fertilizers.

# The Downfall

In 1907, Willson had a summer home built beside Meech Lake, in the Gatineau Hills of Québec. By 1911, he had a power station and a fertilizer factory on his country estate. He carried on inventing there.

*The Willsons' house at Meech Lake.*

*Meech Lake.*

Willson was a very wealthy man, and he owned a great deal of land along the Saguenay River in Québec. But he decided to risk everything to make fertilizers. His scheme failed, and he lost his fortune.

He no longer owned the patents to make calcium carbide in Canada and many other countries. But the patents did not include Newfoundland and Labrador. This region was not part of Canada at that time. So, still undefeated, Willson set about raising funds to build factories there. He did not live to complete his plans. On December 20, 1915, while in New York to raise money, he collapsed and died of a heart attack at age 55.

It is amazing that Willson did so much in his life. He never gave up trying, even when times were very hard. His greatest success, the cheap way of making calcium carbide and acetylene, had a great effect on industry in Canada and around the world. Today, few people have heard of "Carbide" Willson. But he should be remembered as one of the greatest Canadian inventors.

# GLOSSARY

**blacksmith** — A person who makes and repairs iron objects, such as tools and horseshoes. *(p. 4)*

**chemistry** — The study of changes in which materials are changed into other materials. (An example is the study of a wood fire, which changes wood into ash and smoke.) *(p. 4)*

**coal-tar** — A heavy, dark liquid left behind when people **distil** coal. *(p. 10)*

**cotton mill** — A factory where cotton cloth is made from cotton. *(p. 9)*

**distil** — Heat something to boil off a liquid. *(p. 14)*

**fertilizer** — Something added to soil to help plants grow. *(p. 23)*

**formal** — Very polite and well-dressed, but not seeming very friendly. Formal people do not often show their feelings. *(p. 17)*

**furnaces** — Large, very hot ovens. *(p. 7)*

**guarantee a loan** — Help a person to borrow money by promising to repay it if the person does not. *(p. 3)*

**hydro-electricity** — Electricity produced by running water, such as a river or waterfall. *(p. 9)*

**laboratory** — A room where scientists do experiments. *(p. 4)*

**legislature** — A government building where politicians make new laws. *(p. 2)*

**lime** — A white powder made by heating shells, bones, and some kinds of rock. *(p. 10)*

**marine buoys** — Floating objects that show sailors where it is safe or dangerous to go. *(p. 21)*

**mass-produced** — Made in large numbers, usually by machines in factories. *(p. 23)*

**minister** — A person who runs a religious service in a church. *(p. 2)*

**patent** — A way you can register an invention or discovery, so that you are the only person with the right to make or sell it for a certain number of years. *(p. 5)*

**penny-farthing** — A bicycle with a very large front wheel and a very small back wheel. (It was named after two old British coins — the penny, which was large, and the farthing, which was small.) *(p. 7)*

**physics** — The study of certain features of the world around us, such as light, sound, electricity, and how things move. *(p. 4)*

**rivets** — Metal pins that are hammered into place. *(p. 23)*

**soot** — The black powder you see in the smoke from some fires. *(p. 11)*

**transport** — Carry from one place to another. *(p. 15)*

**weld** — Join pieces of metal by heating them and pressing them together. *(p. 23)*

**whale oil** — A kind of oil that comes from the bodies of whales. *(p. 14)*

# INDEX



*1 2 3 4 5 5160-0 95 94 93 92 91*
*1 2 3 4 5 5161-9 95 94 93 92 91*